The Ant and the Grasshopper

This book belongs to _______________

WiSe kids

Writing Upper Case Letters

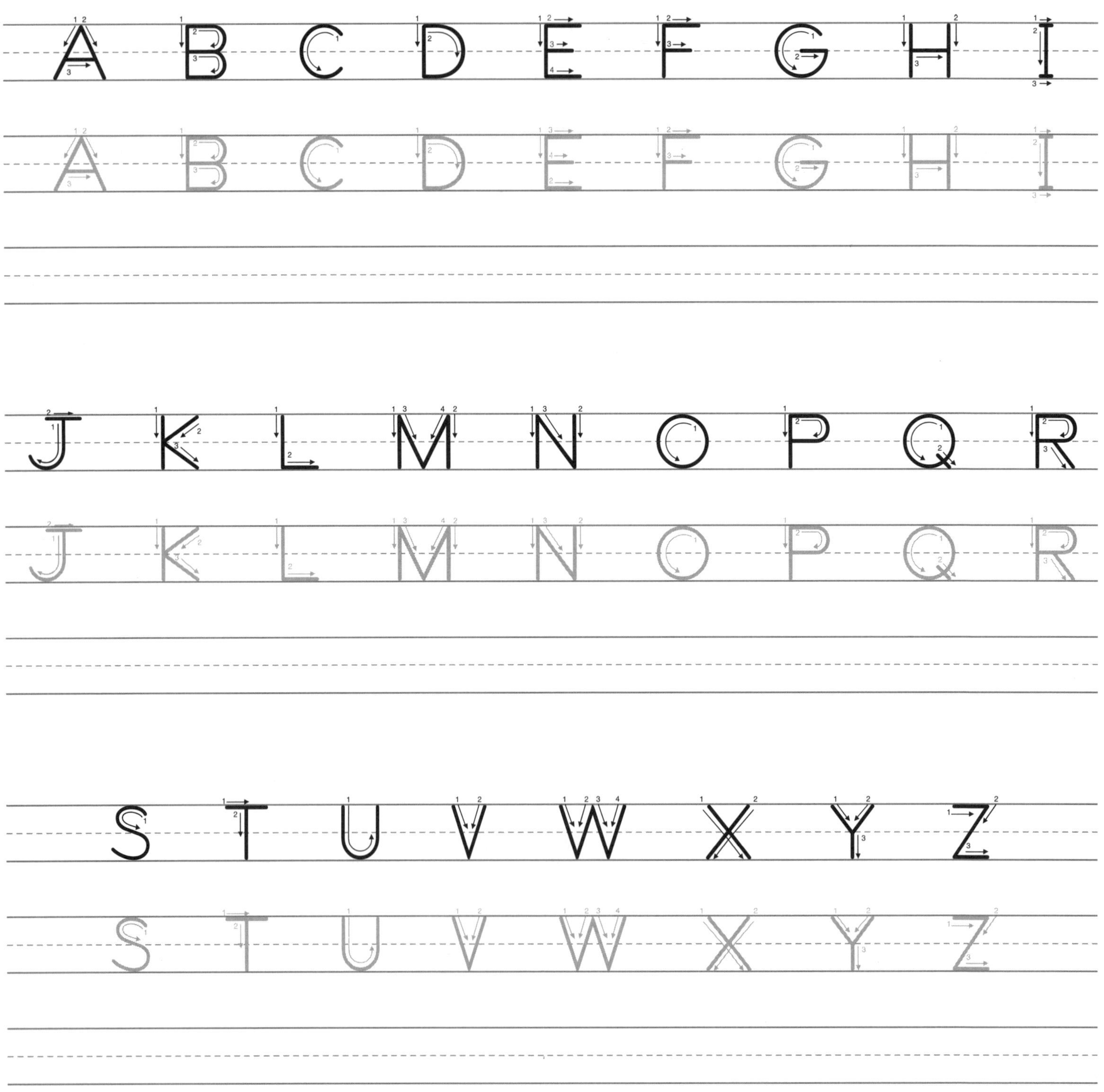

Writing Lower Case Letters

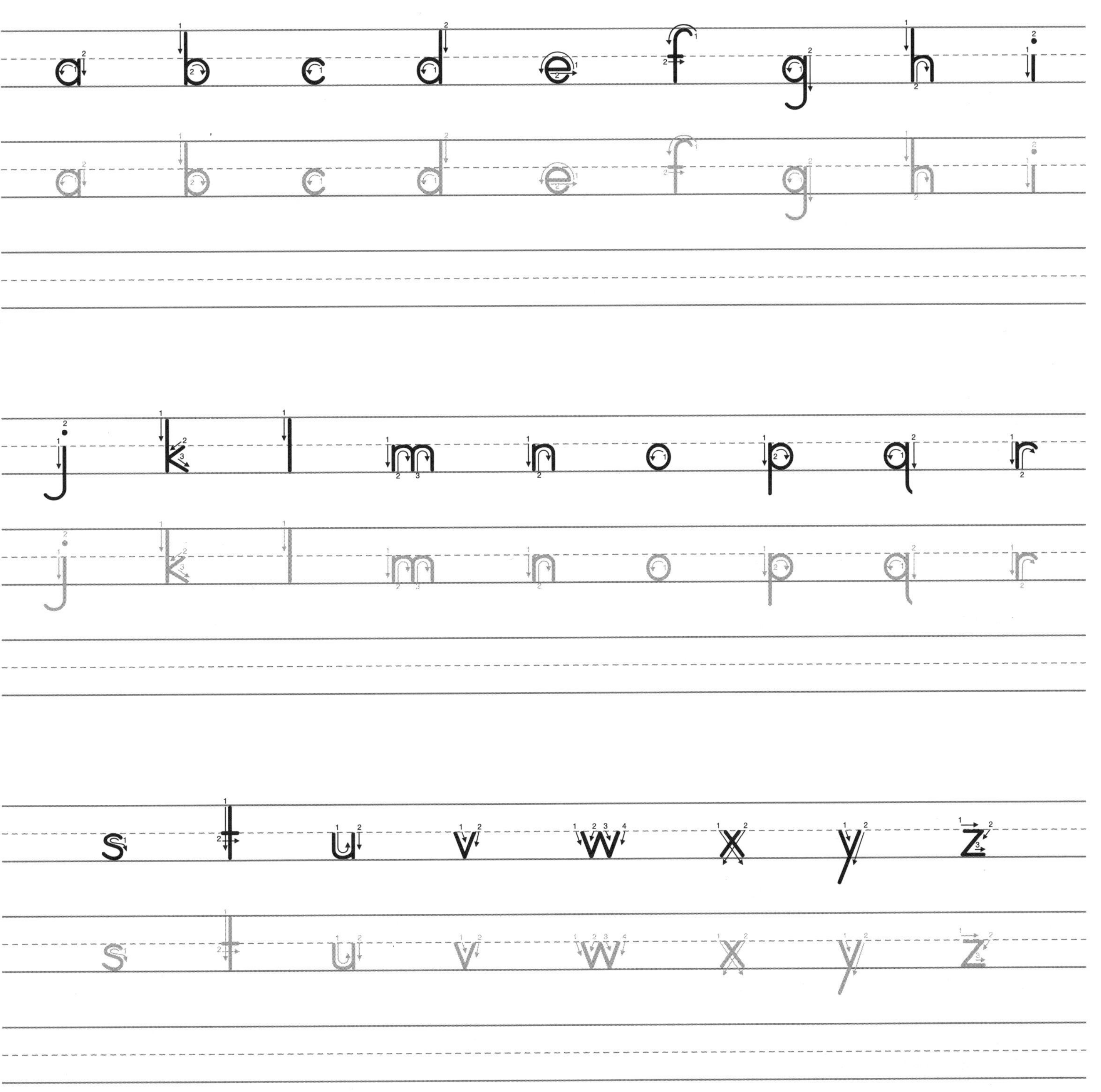

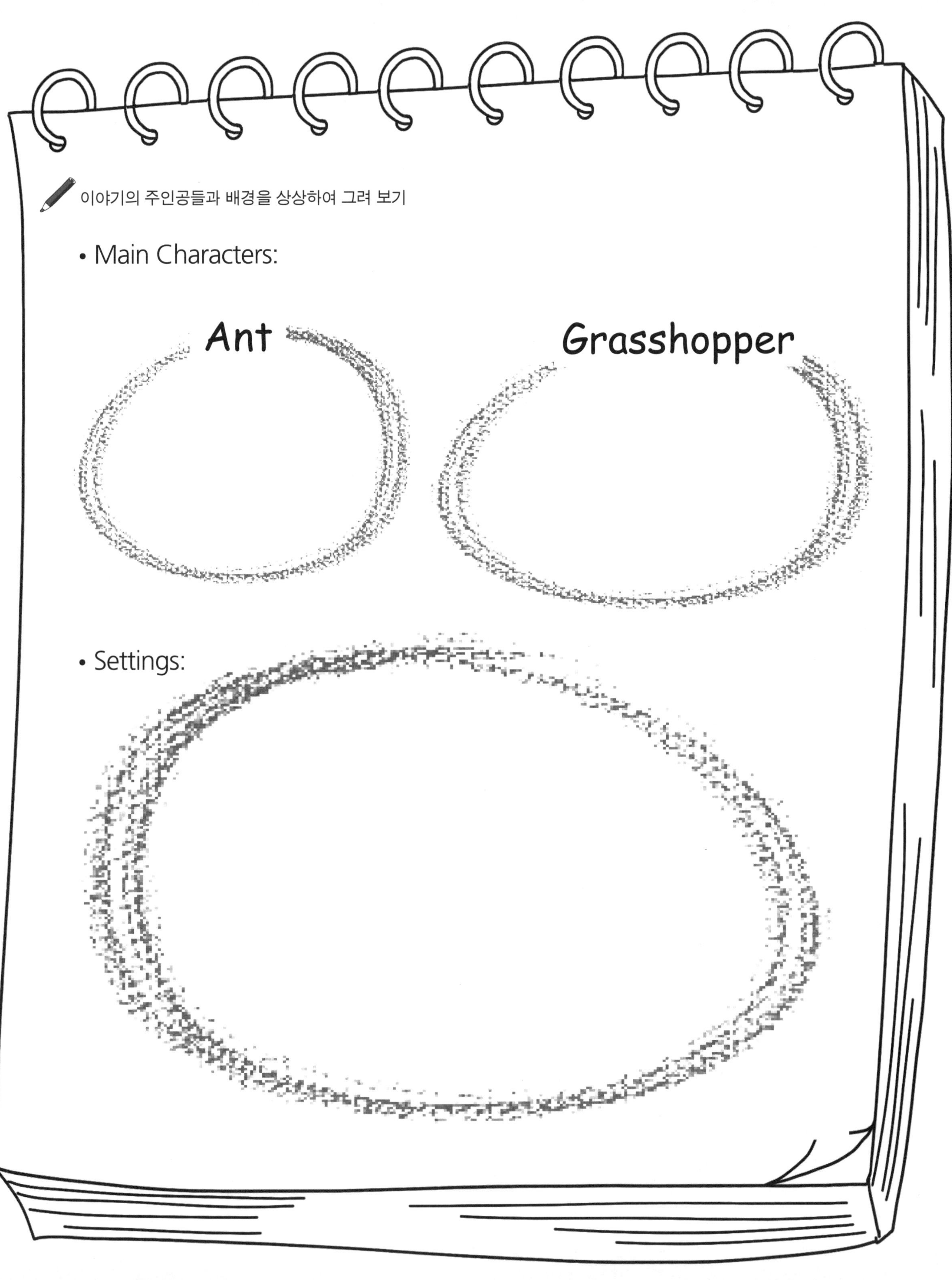
이야기의 주인공들과 배경을 상상하여 그려 보기

• Main Characters:

Ant

Grasshopper

• Settings:

 track 02 그림과 텍스트를 함께 보면서 이야기 듣기

The Ant and the Grasshopper

1

It is summer.

The weather is nice.

Here is a grasshopper in the field.

The grasshopper jumps and sings and dances.

He plays all day long.

2

The weather is getting hot.

Here is an ant in the field.

The ant finds food.

She is busy gathering grain.

She works hard all day long.

3

"Hey, stop working! Come and sing with me."

"No, I can't. Winter is coming soon.

You also should work hard," says the ant.

"Don't be silly! The summer is long."

The grasshopper laughs at the ant.

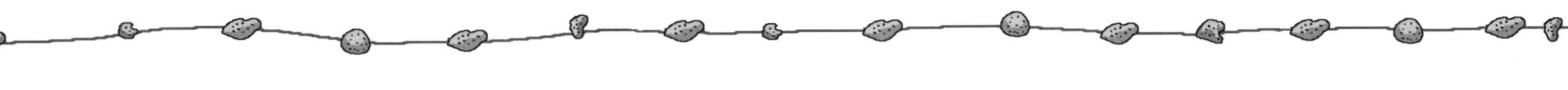

4

Soon it becomes winter.
It snows in the field.
The weather is very cold.
"I can't find any food.
I am hungry," cries the grasshopper.

5

The ant is in her house.
She is warm and happy.
She has lots of food in her house.
She sees the grasshopper outside.
"Oh, poor thing.
I should help him," says the ant.

6

The ant gives him warm food and hot drink.
"Thank you, my friend," says the grasshopper.
"Now, I learned an important thing.
I will work hard in the summer, too."
The grasshopper is deeply sorry.

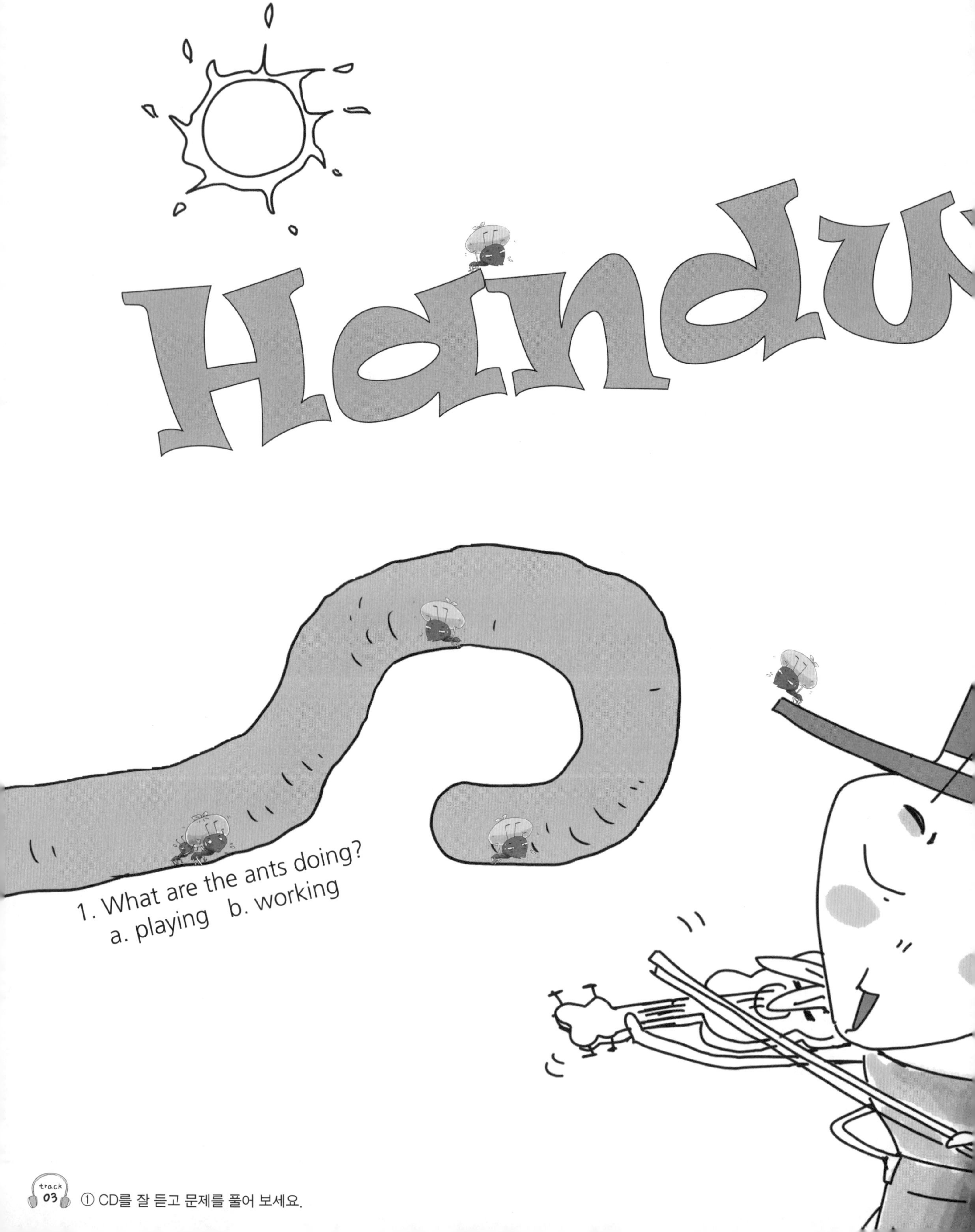

① CD를 잘 듣고 문제를 풀어 보세요.

riting

1st Week

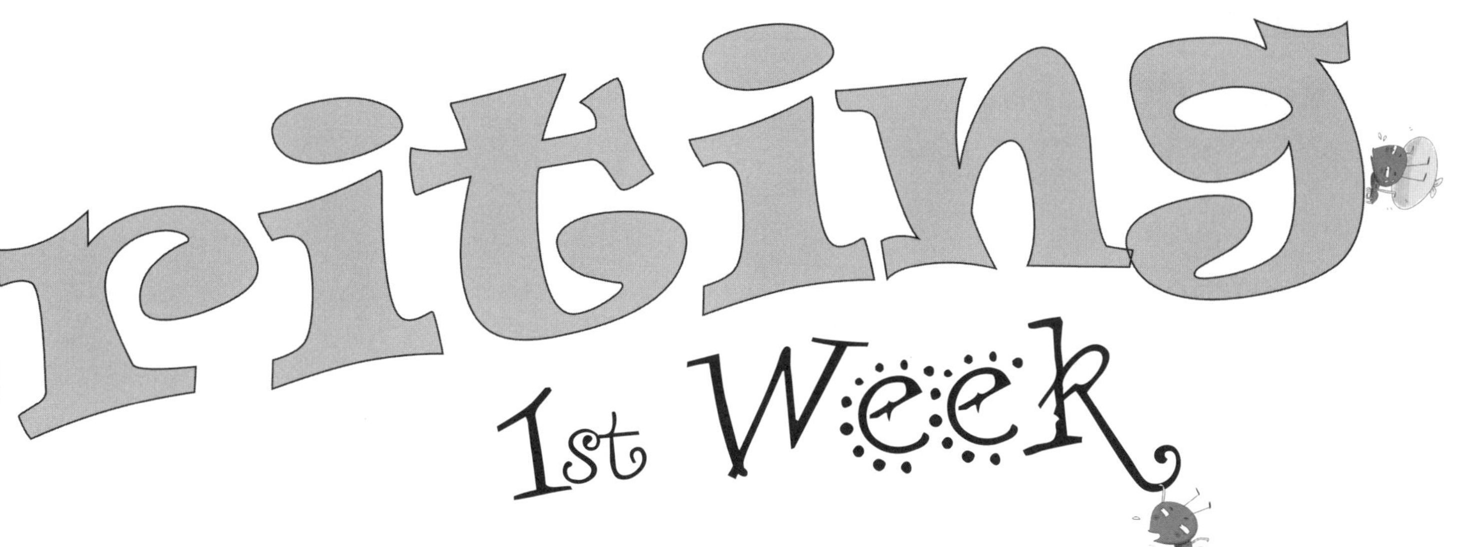

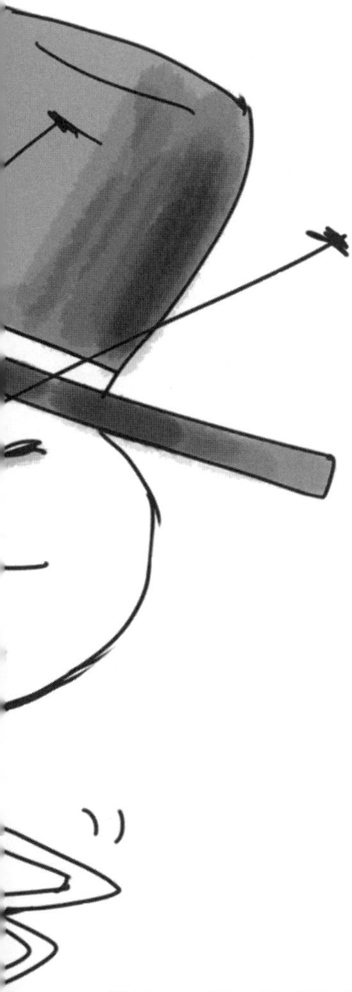

2. What is the grasshopper playing?
a. violin b. piano

② Handwriting 글자를 알록달록 예쁘게 스티커 글자로 꾸며 주세요. 그리고 스티커 개미들도 여기저기 붙여 보세요.

 이야기 들어보기  듣고 따라 읽기

❶ It is summer.//
The weather is nice.//
Here is a grasshopper / in the field.//
The grasshopper jumps / and sings / and dances.//
He plays / all day long.//

❷ The weather is getting hot.//
Here is an ant / in the field.//
The ant finds food.//
She is busy / gathering grain.//
She works hard / all day long.//

❸ "Hey, / stop working!// Come / and sing with me."//
"No, / I can't.// Winter is coming soon.//
You also should work hard,"/ says the ant.//
"Don't be silly!// The summer is long."//
The grasshopper laughs at the ant.//

Key Words

 단어 들어보기  듣고 따라 읽기  단어 써 보기

개미

ant

베짱이

grasshopper

여름

summer

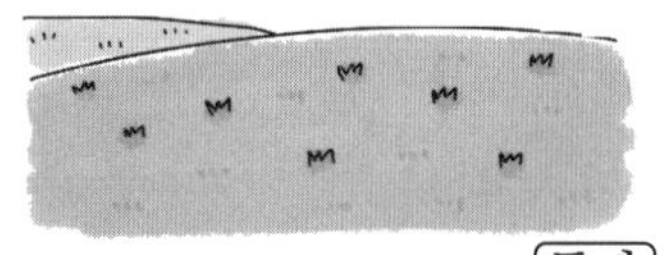
겨울

winter

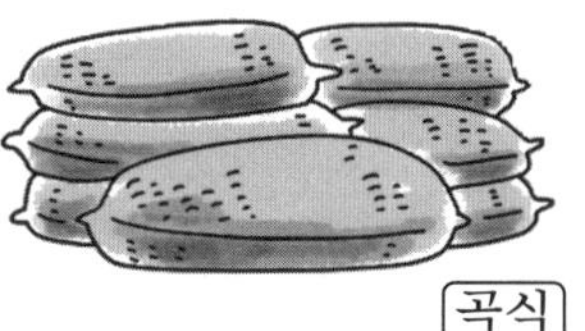
곡식

grain

들판

fietd

더운

hot

뛰어오르다

jump

일하다

work

비웃다

laugh

노래하다

sing

춤추다

dance

 들으면서 끊어 읽기 표시하기　　 듣고 따라 읽기　　✎ 그림자 글씨 따라 쓰기

❶

It is summer. //
여름입니다. //

The weather is nice. //
날씨가 화창합니다. //

Here is a grasshopper / in the field. //
여기 있어요　　베짱이 한 마리가 /　　들판에. //

The grasshopper jumps / and sings / and dances. //
베짱이는 뛰어다닙니다 /　　그리고 노래합니다 /　　그리고 춤을 춥니다. //

He plays / all day long. //
그는 놀아요 /　　하루 종일. //

❷

The weather is getting hot. //
날씨가 점점 더워집니다. //

Here is an ant / in the field. //
여기 있어요　　개미 한 마리가 / 들판에. //

The ant finds food. //
개미는 찾고 있습니다　　음식을 //

She is busy / gathering grain. //
그녀는 바빠요 /　　곡식을 모으느라. //

She works hard / all day long. //
그녀는 열심히 일해요 /　　하루 종일. //

 **3**

"Hey, / stop working! // Come / and sing with me." //
"야, / 일 좀 그만 해! // 이리 와 / 그리고 노래 부르자 나와 함께." //

"No, / I can't. // Winter is coming soon. //
"아니, / 그렇게 할 수 없어. // 겨울이 곧 다가오거든. //

You also should / work hard," / says the ant. //
너도 해야만 해 / 일을 열심히." / 개미가 말합니다. //

"Don't be silly! // The summer is long." //
"멍청하게 굴지 마!" // 여름은 길다고." //

The grasshopper laughs at the ant. //
베짱이는 개미를 비웃습니다. //

Activity

Guess what? and Draw it!

빈 칸에 알맞은 알파벳을 써 보세요. 그 알파벳들을 모아 보면
새로운 단어가 만들어집니다. 찾은 단어의 그림도 스케치북에 그려 보세요.

1) (g)rasshopper

2) summe( )

3) ( )nt

4) f( )eld

5) da( )ce

 Answer (g)( )( )( )( )

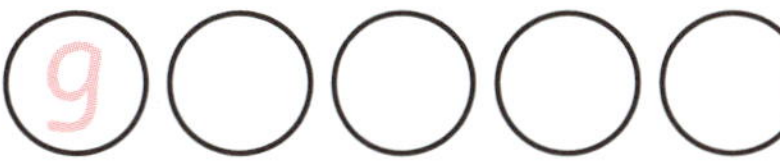

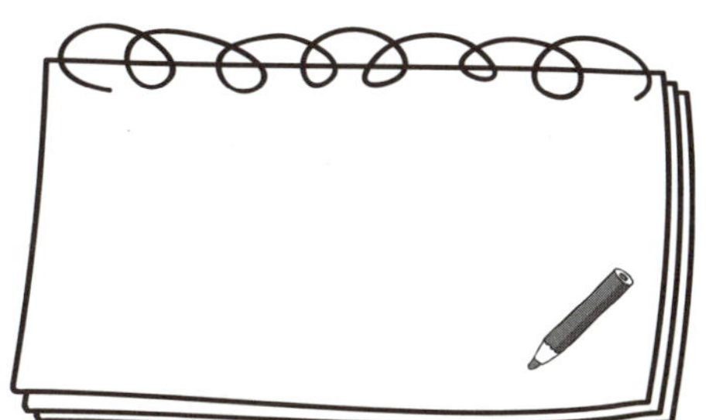

 들으면서 끊어 읽기 표시하기　　 듣고 따라 읽기　　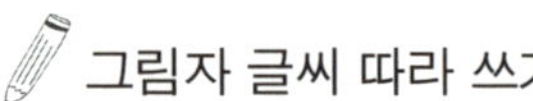 그림자 글씨 따라 쓰기

❶

It is summer. //
여름입니다. //

The weather is nice. //
날씨가 화창합니다. //

Here is a grasshopper / in the field. //
여기 베짱이 한 마리가 있어요 /　　　들판에. //

The grasshopper jumps / and sings / and dances. //
베짱이는 뛰어다닙니다 /　　　그리고 노래합니다 /　　그리고 춤을 춥니다. //

He plays all day long. //
그는 하루 종일 놀아요. //

❷

The weather is getting hot. //
날씨가 점점 더워집니다. //

Here is an ant / in the field. //
여기 개미 한 마리가 있어요. /　들판에. //

The ant finds food. //
개미는 음식을 찾고 있습니다. //

She is busy / gathering grain. //
그녀는 바빠요 /　　곡식을 모으느라. //

She works hard all day long. //
그녀는 하루 종일 열심히 일해요. //

❸

"Hey, stop working! // Come and sing with me." //
"야, 일 좀 그만 해! // 이리 와서 나와 함께 노래 부르자." //

"No, I can't. // Winter is coming soon. //
"아니, 그렇게 할 수 없어. // 겨울이 곧 다가오거든. //

You also should work hard," / says the ant. //
너도 열심히 일 해야만 해." / 개미가 말합니다. //

"Don't be silly! // The summer is long." //
"멍청하게 굴지 마! // 여름은 길다고." //

The grasshopper laughs at the ant. //
베짱이는 개미를 비웃습니다. //

Activity

Unscramble the words!

그림을 잘 보고 주어진 단어들을 이용해서 문장으로 표현해 보세요.

1) 

works   The   day   long
ant   all   hard

The ant ___________________________ .

2) 

ant   the   grasshopper
laughs   The   at

The grasshopper ___________________________ .

Thursday | Whole Story

track 08 이야기 들어보기　　들으면서 동시에 말하기　　✎ 그림자 글씨 따라 쓰기

❶

It is summer.

여름입니다.

The weather is nice.

날씨가 화창합니다.

Here is a grasshopper in the field.

여기 베짱이 한 마리가 있어요　　　들판에.

The grasshopper jumps and sings and dances.

베짱이는 뛰어다닙니다　　　그리고 노래합니다　　그리고 춤을 춥니다.

He plays all day long.

그는 하루 종일 놀아요.

❷

The weather is getting hot.

날씨가 점점 더워집니다.

Here is an ant in the field.

여기 개미 한 마리가 있어요　　들판에.

The ant finds food.

개미는 음식을 찾고 있습니다.

She is busy gathering grain.

그녀는 바빠요　　　곡식을 모으느라.

She works hard all day long.

그녀는 하루 종일 열심히 일해요.

3

"Hey, stop working! Come and sing with me."
"야,　　일 좀 그만 해!　　이리 와서 나와 함께 노래 부르자."

"No, I can't. Winter is coming soon.
"아니, 그렇게 할 수 없어.　겨울이 곧 다가오거든.

You also should work hard," says the ant.
너도 열심히 일 해야만 해."　　개미가 말합니다.

"Don't be silly! The summer is long."
"멍청하게 굴지 마!　여름은 길다고."

The grasshopper laughs at the ant.
베짱이는 개미를 비웃습니다.

Activity

Secret Message 탐정이 범인을 찾을 수 있도록 도와주세요!
빈 칸에 알맞은 단어들을 써 보면 범인이 어디에 있는지 알 수 있어요.

1) The ant finds ●○○○.

2) Here ●○ a grasshopper.

3) Come and sing with ○●.

4) The summer is ●○○○.

5) He plays all ●○○ long.

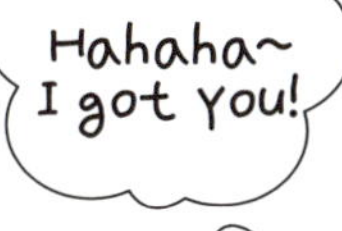

Answer　●●●●●

track 09 이야기 들어보기   들으면서 빈칸 채우기

①

It is ______ .

______ ______ is ______ .

Here ______ a ______ ______ ______ ______ .

______ grasshopper ______ ______ and ______ .

He ______ all ______ ______ .

②

The ______ is ______ ______ .

______ is ant the ______ .

______ ______ ______ food.

______ is ______ ______ grain.

She ______ ______ day ______ .

3

"Hey, ████ ████ ! and sing ████ ████ ."

"No, ████ . ████ is ████ soon.

You also ████ work ████ ," ████ the ant.

" ████ silly! ████ summer ████ ████ ."

████ grasshopper ████ ████ ant.

Grammar Activity

Circle the correct word.

알맞은 단어를 찾아 동그라미 하세요.

1. (I, My, Me) see (a , an) grasshopper.
2. (He, His, Him) plays the violin.
3. (I, My, Me) see (a , an) ant.
4. (She, Her, Hers) works.
5. "Come and sing with (I, my, me)!"
6. "No, I can't. (You, Your, Yours) also should work hard."

Fill in the blanks. 빈 칸에 알맞은 단어를 고르세요.

1. The grasshopper plays in the ___________ .
   a. spring   b. summer   c. fall   d. winter

2. The ___________ is nice.
   a. sky   b. ant   c. grasshopper   d. weather

3. The ant is busy ___________ grain.
   a. eating   b. playing   c. gathering   d. dancing

4. The grasshopper says, "The summer is ___________."
   a. short   b. long   c. happy   d. sad

True or False? 내용이 맞으면 T, 틀리면 F 에 동그라미 하세요.

5. The ant plays all day long.   T / F

6. The grasshopper laughs at the ant.   T / F

Complete the words. 올바른 단어가 되도록 연결해 보세요.

7. sum   •   • hopper

8. fie   •   • mer

9. wea   •   • ther

10. grass   •   • ld

11. __________________________

- "You also should work hard."
- "Winter is coming soon."

12. __________________________

- "Don't be silly!"
- "Come and sing with me."

Match the sentences to the pictures. 다음 그림을 올바르게 설명하고 있는 문장을 고르세요.

13. a. The grasshopper jumps and sings.

b. The grasshopper dances and works.

14. a. The ant eats food and works hard.

b. The ant finds food and works hard.

15. a. The weather is hot.

b. The weather is very cold.

① CD를 잘 듣고 문제를 풀어 보세요.

riting

2nd Week

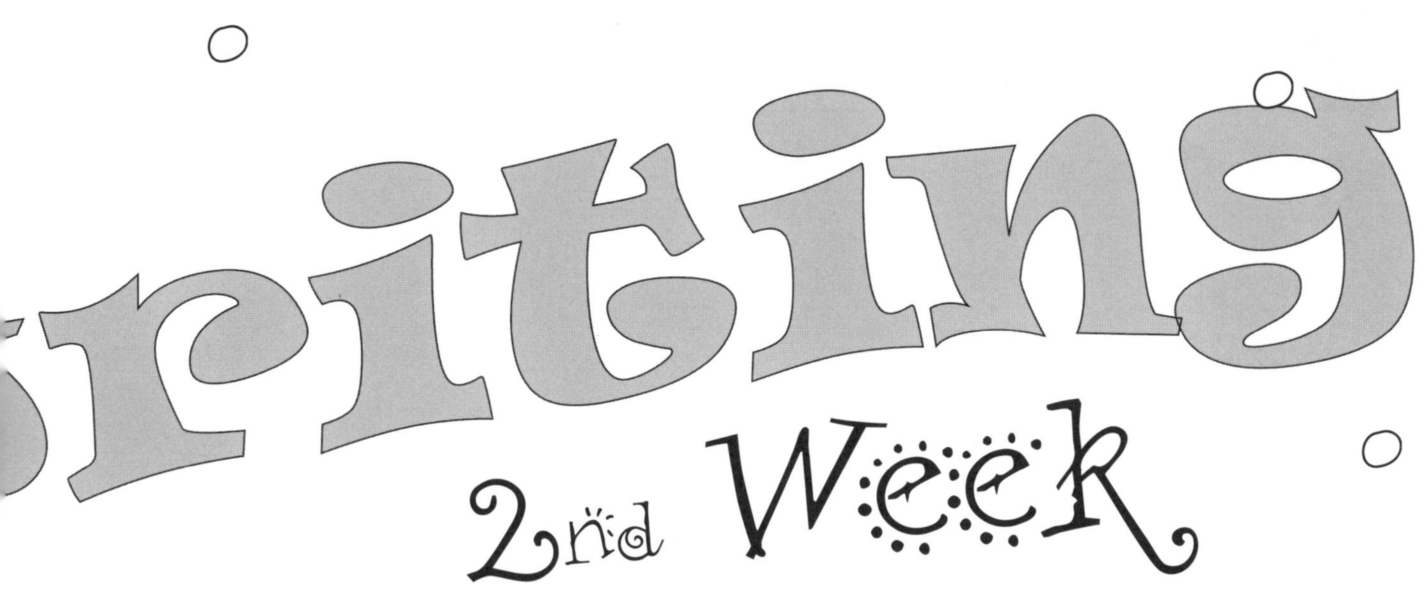

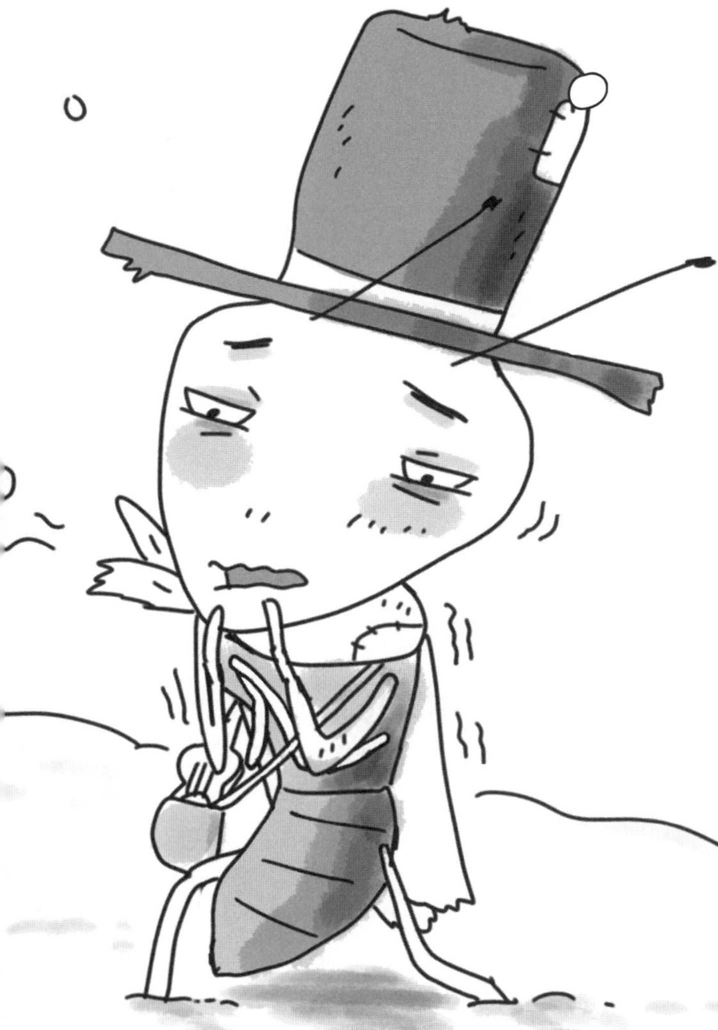

1. How is the weather?
   a. hot   b. cold

2. Where is a 'snowman'? Find it and circle it.

② 추위에 떨고 있는 베짱이를 mittens earmuffs boots 스티커로 따뜻하게 입혀 주세요.

이야기 들어보기   듣고 따라 읽기

❹ Soon / it becomes winter. //
It snows / in the field. //
The weather is very cold. //
"I can't find any food. //
I am hungry," / cries the grasshopper. //

❺ The ant is / in her house. //
She is warm / and happy. //
She has lots of food / in her house. //
She sees the grasshopper / outside. //
"Oh, / poor thing. //
I should help him," / says the ant. //

❻ The ant gives him warm food / and hot drink. //
"Thank you, / my friend," / says the grasshopper. //
"Now, / I learned an important thing. //
I will work hard / in the summer, too." //
The grasshopper is deeply sorry. //

Key Words

사인해 주세요
track 12 단어 들어보기   듣고 따라 읽기   단어 써 보기
snow
눈이 오다
cold
추운
drink
마실것
warm
따뜻한
house
집
outside
밖에
hungry
배고픈
poor
불쌍한
important
중요한
sorry
후회하는
find
찾다
help
돕다

 들으면서 끊어 읽기 표시하기    듣고 따라 읽기   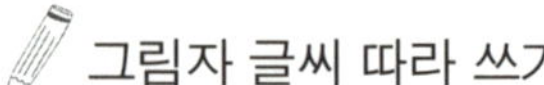 그림자 글씨 따라 쓰기

Soon /it becomes winter. //
머지않아 /   겨울이 됩니다. //

It snows /in the field. //
눈이 옵니다 /   들판에. //

The weather is very cold. //
날씨가 매우 추워요. //

"I can't find any food. //
"나는 찾을 수가 없어   어떤 음식도. //

I am hungry," /cries the grasshopper. //
나는 배가 고파." /   베짱이가 흐느낍니다. //

The ant is /in her house. //
개미가 있네요 /   그녀의 집 안에. //

She is warm /and happy. //
그녀는 따뜻해요 /   그리고 행복합니다. //

She has lots of food /in her house. //
그녀는 가지고 있어요 많은 음식을 /   그녀의 집 안에. //

She sees the grasshopper /outside. //
그녀가 봅니다   베짱이를 /   밖에 있는. //

"Oh, /poor thing. // I should help him," /says the ant. //
"어머, /   불쌍해라. //   난 해야만 해   그를 도와야겠어." /   개미가 말합니다. //

6

The ant gives him warm food / and hot drink. //

개미는 그에게 줍니다　　　　따뜻한 음식을 /　　　　그리고 뜨거운 마실 것을. //

"Thank you, / my friend," / says the grasshopper. //

"고마워, /　　　　나의 친구야." /　　　　베짱이가 말합니다. //

"Now, / I learned an important thing. //

"이제, /　　　난 배웠어　　　중요한 것을 말이야. //

I will work hard / in the summer, too." //

난 열심히 일할 거야 /　　　　여름에도." //

The grasshopper is deeply sorry. //

베짱이는 깊이 후회합니다. //

Activity

Word Search

다음 단어들을 찾아 보세요. 그리고 얼마나 시간이 걸리는지도 체크해 보세요.

a	d	f	k	s	n	o	w
i	b	c	h	e	l	h	a
p	m	c	o	l	d	t	r
s	b	h	u	j	p	y	m
o	o	w	s	l	s	g	q
r	n	a	e	u	f	d	j
r	c	h	u	n	g	r	y
y	x	g	z	e	i	v	r

~~warm~~
help
snow
cold
house
sorry
hungry

How long did it take to finish them all? _______ min. ______ sec.

 들으면서 끊어 읽기 표시하기　 듣고 따라 읽기　 그림자 글씨 따라 쓰기

4

Soon / it becomes winter. //

머지않아 /　겨울이 됩니다. //

It snows in the field. //

들판에 눈이 옵니다. //

The weather is very cold. //

날씨가 매우 추워요. //

"I can't find any food. //

"나는 어떤 음식도 찾을 수가 없어. //

I am hungry." / cries the grasshopper. //

나는 배가 고파." /　　베짱이가 흐느낍니다. //

5

The ant is in her house. //

개미가 그녀의 집 안에 있습니다. //

She is warm / and happy. //

그녀는 따뜻해요 /　그리고 행복합니다. //

She has lots of food / in her house. //

개미는 많은 음식을 가지고 있어요 /　그녀의 집 안에. //

She sees the grasshopper / outside. //

개미가 베짱이를 봅니다 /　밖에 있는. //

"Oh, poor thing. // I should help him." / says the ant. //

"어머,　불쌍해라. //　내가 그를 도와야겠어." /　개미가 말합니다. //

6

The ant gives him warm food / and hot drink. //

개미는 그에게 따뜻한 음식을 줍니다 /   그리고 뜨거운 마실 것을. //

"Thank you, my friend," / says the grasshopper. //

"고마워,   나의 친구야." /   베짱이가 말합니다. //

"Now, / I learned an important thing. //

"이제, /   난 중요한 것을 배웠어. //

I will work hard / in the summer, too." //

난 열심히 일할 거야 /   여름에도." //

The grasshopper is deeply sorry. //

베짱이는 깊이 후회합니다. //

Activity

Guess What?

Q. Why does the ant help the grasshopper?

다음 단어들을 올바르게 바꿔 써 보면, 답을 찾을 수 있어요.

1) elidf   f i e l d (1)

2) opor   _ _ _ ☐(2)

3) vgie   _ ☐(3) _ _

4) naler   _ ☐(4) _ _ _

5) uhgryn   _ _ ☐(5) _ _ _

6) ldoc   _ _ _ ☐(6)

A. Because she thinks that he is her f ☐(1) ☐(2) ☐(3) ☐(4) ☐(5) ☐(6) .

  이야기 들어보기   들으면서 동시에 말하기   그림자 글씨 따라 쓰기

4

Soon it becomes winter.

머지않아 겨울이 됩니다.

It snows in the field.

들판에 눈이 옵니다.

The weather is very cold.

날씨가 매우 추워요.

"I can't find any food.

"나는 어떤 음식도 찾을 수가 없어.

I am hungry," cries the grasshopper.

나는 배가 고파."   베짱이가 흐느낍니다.

5

The ant is in her house.

개미가 집 안에 있습니다.

She is warm and happy.

그녀는 따뜻하고 행복합니다.

She has lots of food in her house.

그녀는 그녀의 집 안에 많은 음식을 가지고 있어요.

She sees the grasshopper outside.

그녀가 밖에 있는 베짱이를 봅니다.

"Oh, poor thing. I should help him," says the ant.

"어머, 불쌍해라.   내가 그를 도와야겠어."   개미가 말합니다.

6

The ant gives him warm food and hot drink.

개미는 그에게 따뜻한 음식과 뜨거운 마실것을 줍니다.

"Thank you, my friend," says the grasshopper.

"고마워, 나의 친구야."   베짱이가 말합니다.

"Now, I learned an important thing.

"이제, 난 아주 중요한 것을 배웠어.

I will work hard in the summer, too."

난 열심히 여름에도 일할 거야.

The grasshopper is deeply sorry.

베짱이는 깊이 후회합니다.

Activity

Can you find them?

각 문제에서 말하는 것을 찾아 주어진 모양으로 표시해 보세요.

1) Find three cups and draw a star.

2) Find the hat and draw a triangle .

3) Find the table and draw a square.

4) Find the window and draw a rectangle.

5) Find the kettle and draw a diamond.

 star  triangle  square  rectangle  diamond

1

______ it ______ ______ .

______ ______ the field.

The ______ very ______ .

"I ______ ______ food.

______ hungry," ______ the grasshopper.

2

The ______ ______ ______ house.

______ warm ______ happy.

She ______ ______ in her ______ .

She ______ the ______ ______ .

"Oh, ______ ______ ______ ______ him," says the ant.

3

The ant ▊▊▊ food and ▊▊ .

" ▊▊ you, my ▊▊ ," ▊▊ the grasshopper.

" ▊▊ , I ▊▊ an ▊▊ ▊▊ .

I ▊▊ ▊▊ in the ▊▊ , too."

The grasshopper ▊▊ ▊▊ .

Grammar Activity

Circle the correct word.

알맞은 단어를 찾아 동그라미 하세요.

1) I (am, are, is) in the house.

2) She (am, are, is) warm and happy.

3) The grasshoper (am, are, is) cold and hungry.

4) It (am, are, is) nice and cool.

5) The ant (am, are, is) in the field.

6) We (am, are, is) friends.

7) They (am, are, is) not hungry now.

Fill in the blanks. 빈 칸에 알맞은 단어를 고르세요.

1. The ant has lots of ___________ in her house.

   a. food   b. friends   c. money   d. snow

2. The ant gives the grasshopper hot___________.

   a. money   b. snow   c. food   d. drink

3. The grasshopper is deeply ___________.

   a. happy   b. sorry   c. poor   d. angry

4. The grasshopper will ___________ hard next summer.

   a. play   b. sing   c. work   d. dance

True or False? 내용이 맞으면 T, 틀리면 F 에 동그라미 하세요.

5. The grasshopper sees the ant outside.   T / F

6. The ant helps the grasshopper.   T / F

Complete the sentences. 다음 단어들을 이용하여 문장을 완성하세요.

7. learned, Now, an, thing, I, important

   ____.

8. food, and, drink, hot, She, him, gives, warm

   ____.

9. **Put the sentences in order.** 다음 문장들을 일어난 순서대로 다시 써 보세요.

> a. The ant finds food and works hard.
>
> b. The grasshopper can't find any food.
>
> c. The grasshopper jumps and sings and dances.
>
> d. The grasshopper is deeply sorry.
>
> e. The ant sees the grasshopper outside.
>
> f. The ant gives him warm food and hot drink.

c The grasshopper

10. **The lesson of this story** 이 이야기의 교훈은 무엇인가요?

a. Always be happy.　　　　b. Prepare for tomorrow.

c. Help your friends.　　　　d. Work hard all day long.

✏️ 해석을 읽고 영어로 옮겨 보기

❶

여름입니다.

날씨가 화창합니다.

여기 베짱이 한 마리가 들판에 있어요.

베짱이는 뛰어다니고 노래하며 춤을 춥니다.

그는 하루 종일 놉니다.

❷

날씨가 점점 더워집니다.

여기 개미 한 마리가 들판에 있어요.

개미는 음식을 찾고 있습니다.

그녀는 곡식을 모으느라 바빠요.

그녀는 하루 종일 열심히 일해요.

3

"야, 일 좀 그만 해! 이리 와서 나랑 노래 부르자."

"아니, 그렇게 할 수 없어. 겨울이 곧 다가오거든.

너도 열심히 일 해야만 해." 개미가 말합니다.

"멍청하게 굴지 마! 여름은 길다고."

베짱이는 개미를 비웃습니다.

4

머지않아 겨울이 됩니다.

들판에 눈이 옵니다.

날씨가 매우 추워요.

"나는 어떤 음식도 찾을 수가 없어.

나는 배가 고파." 베짱이가 흐느낍니다.

❺

개미가 집 안에 있습니다.

그녀는 따뜻하고 행복합니다.

그녀는 많은 음식을 그녀의 집 안에 가지고 있어요.

그녀가 밖에 있는 베짱이를 봅니다.

"어머, 불쌍해라. 내가 그를 도와야겠어." 개미가 말합니다.

❻

개미는 베짱이에게 따뜻한 음식과 뜨거운 마실것을 줍니다.

"고마워, 나의 친구야." 베짱이가 말합니다.

"이제, 난 중요한 것을 배웠어.

여름에도 난 열심히 일할 거야."

베짱이는 깊이 후회합니다.

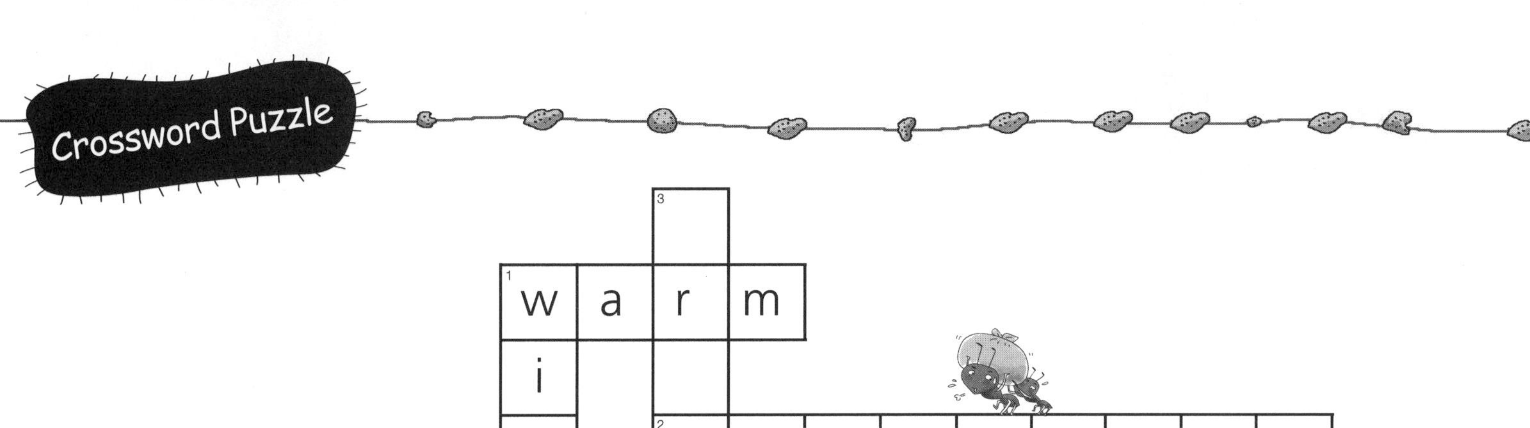

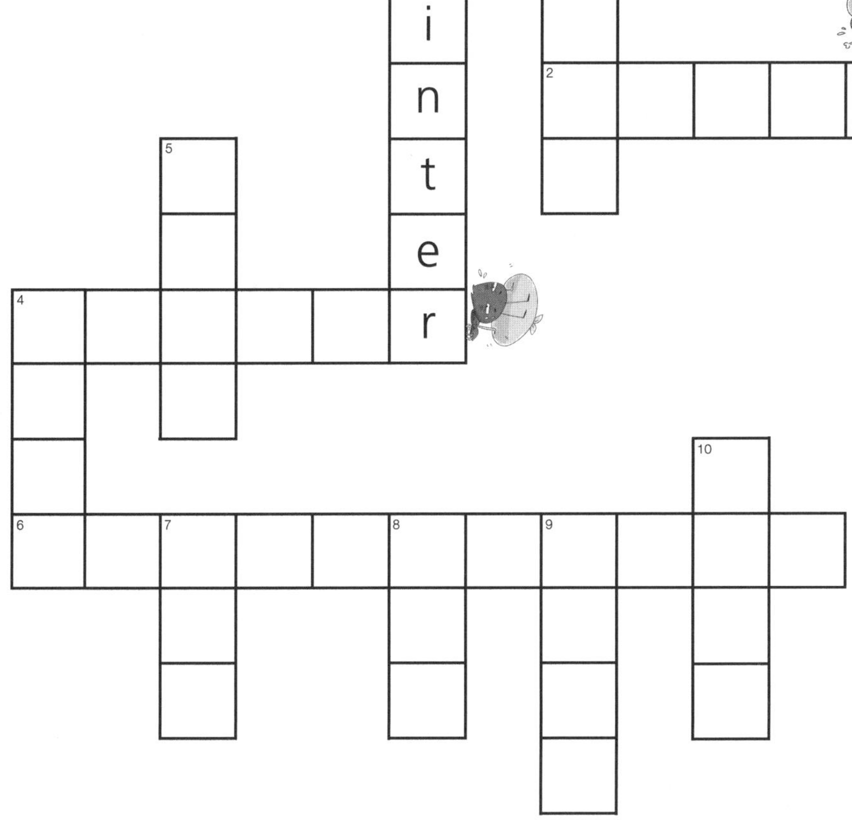

1 She is __warm__ and happy.

2 I learned an ____________ thing.

4 It is ____________.

6 The ____________ is deeply sorry.

1 ____winter____

3 ____________

4 ____________

5 ____________

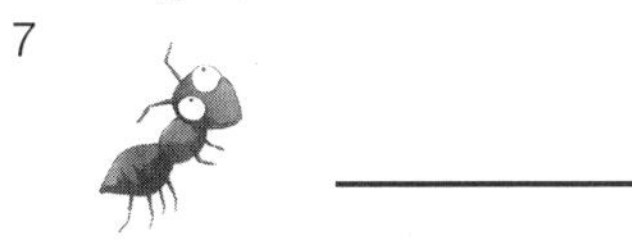
7 ____________

8 ____________

9 ____________

10 ____________

* 정답은 홈페이지 www.screenplay.co.kr에서 확인할 수 있습니다.

blackboard 칠판
important
chalk 분필

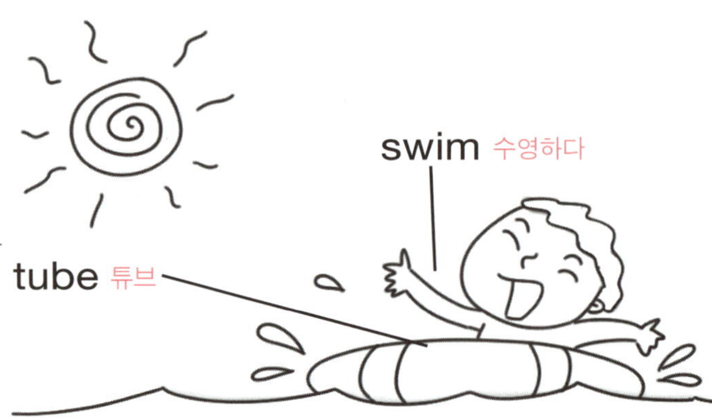
swim 수영하다
tube 튜브

handkerchief 손수건
scarf 스카프
hot 더운

hat 모자
microphone 마이크
sing 노래하다

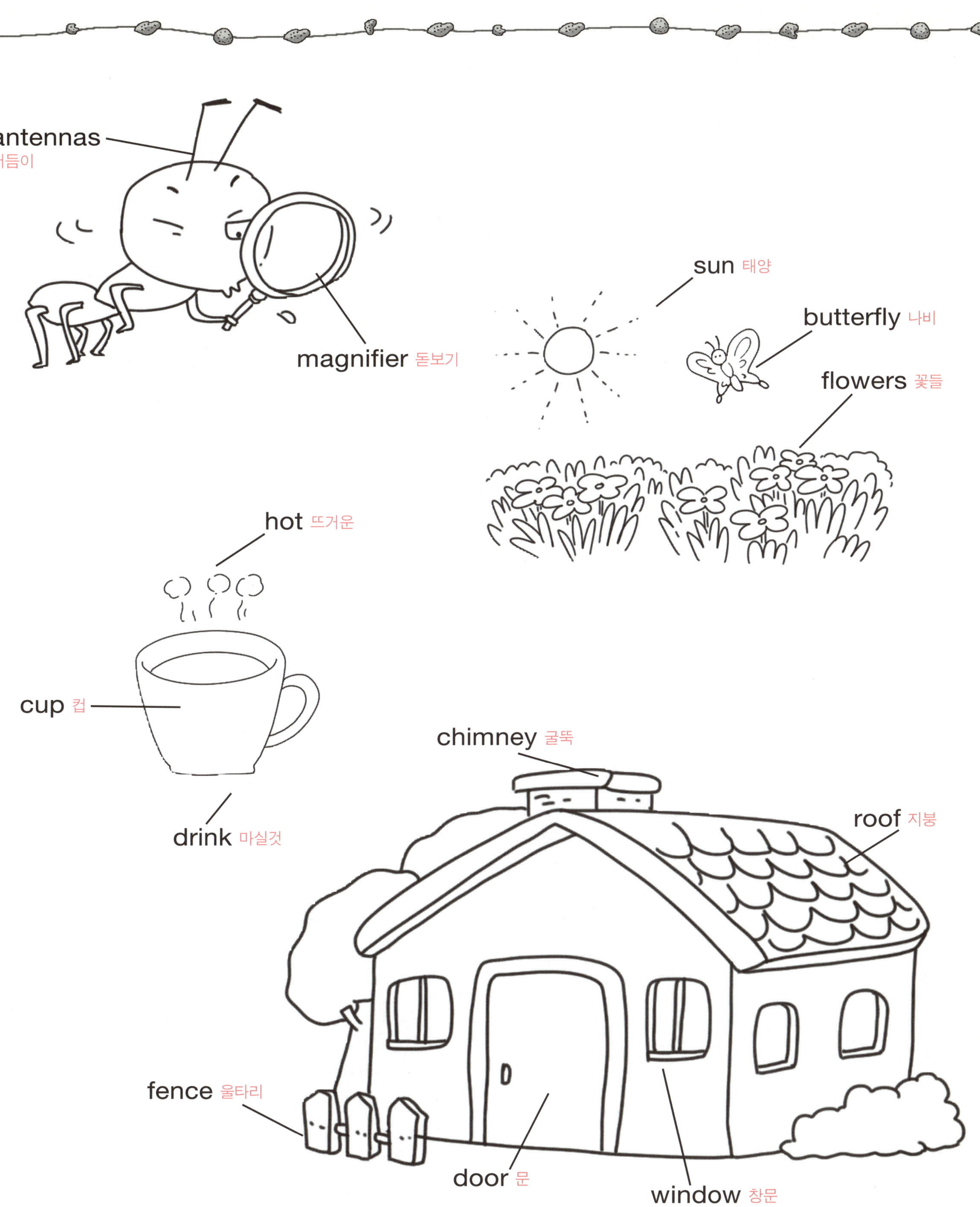

antennas
더듬이
magnifier 돋보기
sun 태양
butterfly 나비
flowers 꽃들
hot 뜨거운
cup 컵
drink 마실것
chimney 굴뚝
roof 지붕
fence 울타리
door 문
window 창문

Answers 1st Week

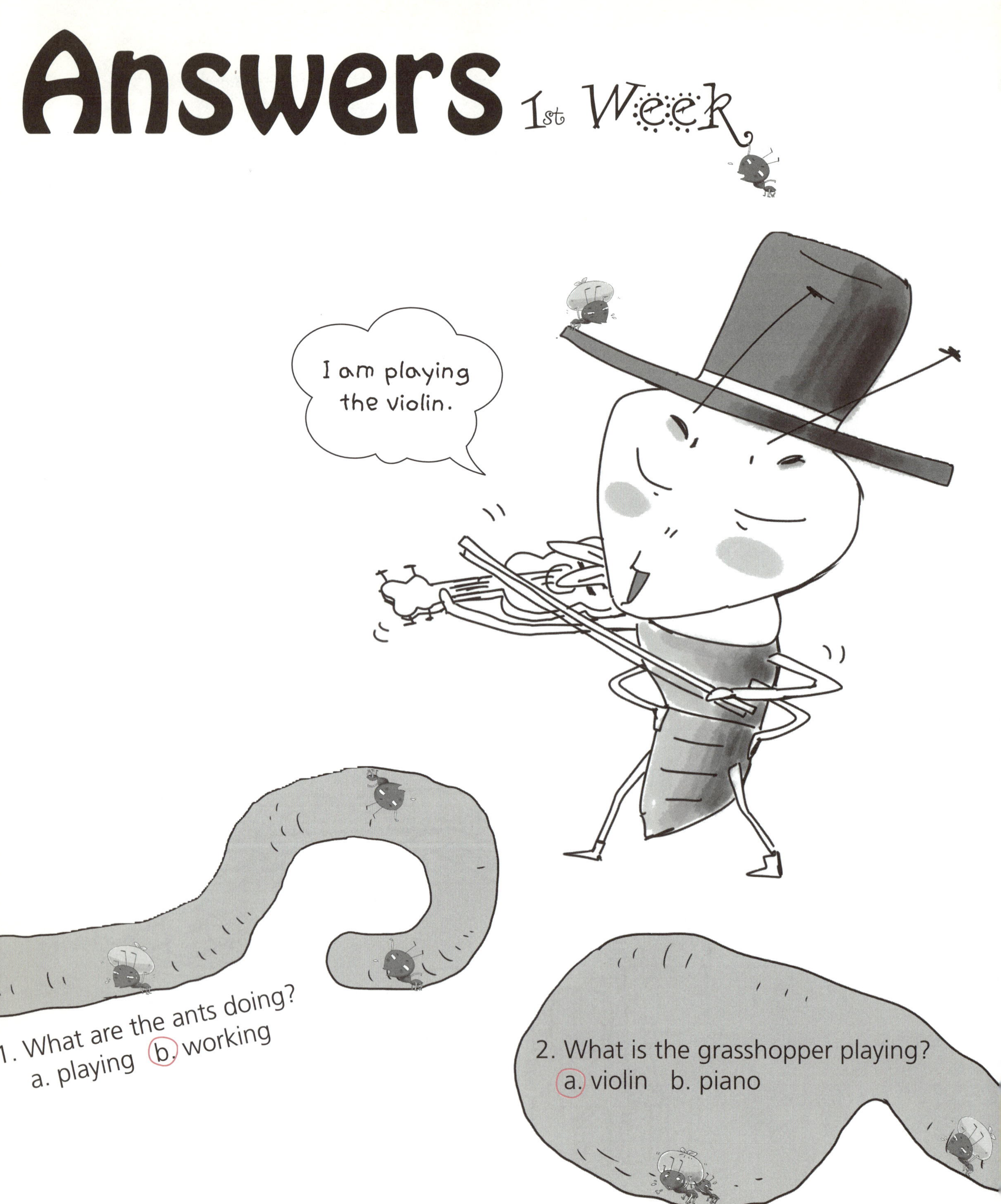

Activity p.13

Guess what? and Draw it!

1) (g)rasshopper
2) summe (r)
3) (a)nt
4) f (i) eld
5) da (n) ce

Answer (g) (r) (a) (i) (n)

Activity p.15

Unscramble the words!

1) works   The   day   long   ant   all   hard

The ant works hard all day long.

2) ant   the   grasshopper   laughs   The   at

The grasshopper laughs at the ant.

Activity p.17

🔍 Secret Message

1) The ant finds (f) (o) (o) (d).
2) Here (i) (s) a grasshopper.
3) Come and sing with (m) (e).
4) The summer is (l) (o) (n) (g).
5) He plays all (d) (a) (y) long.

Answer (f) (i) (e) (l) (d)

Activity p.19

Circle the correct word.

1. (I, My, Me) see (a, an) grasshopper.
2. (He, His, Him) plays the violin.
3. (I, My, Me) see (a, an) ant.
4. (She, Her, Hers) works.
5. "Come and sing with (I, my, me)!"
6. "No, I can't. (You, Your, Yours) also should work hard."

Fill in the blanks.

1. ⓑ The grasshopper plays in the <u>summer</u>.

2. ⓓ The <u>weather</u> is nice.

3. ⓒ The ant is busy <u>gathering</u> grain.

4. ⓑ The summer is <u>long</u>.

True or False?

5. The ant plays all day long.   T /(F)

6. The grasshopper laughs at the ant.   (T)/ F

Complete the words.

7. summer   8. field   9. weather   10. grasshopper

Who said that?

11. Ant   12. Grasshopper

Match the sentences to the pictures.

13. ⓐ The grasshopper jumps and sings.

14. ⓑ The ant finds food and works hard.

15. ⓑ The weather is very cold.

Answers 2nd Week

Activity p.27

Word Search

a	d	f	k	s	n	o	w
i	b	c	h	e	l	h	a
p	m	c	o	l	d	t	r
s	b	h	u	j	p	y	m
o	o	w	s	l	s	g	q
r	n	a	e	u	f	d	j
r	c	h	u	n	g	r	y
y	x	g	z	e	i	v	r

warm
help
snow
cold
house
sorry
hungry

How long did it take to finish them all? _____ min. _____ sec.

Activity p.29

Guess What?

Q. Why does the ant help the grasshopper?

1) elidf — f i e l d (1)

2) opor — p o o r (2)

3) vgie — g i v e (3)

4) naler — l e a r n (4)

5) uhgryn — h u n g r y (5)

6) ldoc — c o l d (6)

A. Because she thinks that he is her f r i e n d. (1) (2) (3) (4) (5) (6)

Activity p.31

Can you find them?

Grammar Activity p.33

Circle the correct word.

1) I (am, are, is) in the house.
2) She (am, are, is) warm and happy.
3) The grasshoper (am, are, is) cold and hungry.
4) It (am, are, is) nice and cool.
5) The ant (am, are, is) in the field.
6) We (am, are, is) friends.
7) They (am, are, is) not hungry now.

Fill in the blanks.

1. ⓐ The ant has lots of <u>food</u> in her house.

2. ⓓ The ant gives the grasshopper hot <u>drink</u>.

3. ⓑ The grasshopper is deeply <u>sorry</u>.

4. ⓒ The grasshopper will <u>work</u> next summer.

True or False?

5. The grasshopper sees the ant outside.　　　　T /(F)

6. The ant helps the grasshopper.　　　　(T)/ F

Complete the sentences.

7. Now, I learned an important thing.

8. She gives him warm food and hot drink.

Put the sentences in order.

9. c The grasshopper jumps and sings and dances.
   a The ant finds food and works hard.
   b The grasshopper can't find any food.
   e The ant sees the grasshopper outside.
   f The ant gives him warm food and hot drink.
   d The grasshopper is deeply sorry.

The lesson of this story.

10. ⓑ Prepare for tomorrow.

2009년부터 실시된 8차 교육과정의 핵심 중 하나는 바로 '문자지도와 어휘 수의 확대' 입니다. 그동안 말하기와 듣기 등 음성언어 지도에만 치중해 왔던 7차 교육과정에 따른 부족함을 보완하기 위한 방안이라고 볼 수 있는데요. 사실 우리나라와 같은 환경에서는 음성언어보다는 문자를 통해 의사소통을 해야 하는 경우가 더 많은데, 그 동안 문자지도는 경시되어 왔습니다.

진정한 '쓰기' 란 단어나 문장 한 개를 쓰는 것을 의미하지 않습니다. 보다 큰 단위의 한 가지 이상의 내용들이 명확한 글로 표현 되어 의사소통이 원활하게 이루어질 때, 그것을 '쓰기' 라고 할 수 있습니다. 'Handwriting' 연습노트 시리즈는 어린 학습자가 그러한 진정한 쓰기를 자유롭게 할 수 있도록 체계적인 훈련을 바탕으로 특별히 **'문자지도 어휘 강화 프로그램'** 입니다. 학습자의 레벨에 따라 단계를 선택하여, 하루 20분 정도 월요일부터 토요일까지 순차적으로 반복, 수정과정을 거치면서 기억력을 강화시켜 나간다면, 이 자체만으로도 아이가 갖게 되는 성취감은 클 것입니다.

Step 1: Warm Up

Picture Reading
이야기 상상 단계
그림만 봐도 내용을 알 수 있죠. 드라마틱하게 녹음된 내용을 들으면서 이야기 속으로 빠져 보세요.

Characters & Settings
주인공과 배경 알기
주인공과 배경을 파악할 수 있도록 도와주세요. 굳이 영어로 표현하지 않아도 괜찮습니다. 그림으로 나타낼 수 있도록 해 주세요.

Storytelling
그림과 글을 함께 보면서 듣기
그림책을 보듯 편안하게 이야기를 듣도록 해 주세요. 이 때 함께 글을 손으로 짚어가면서 들어도 좋습니다. 아이가 "이게 무슨 뜻이야?" 라고 물어본다면, 직접 추측해 보도록 도와주세요.

Step 2: Main Study

Monday
Listen and Read / Key Words 주요 단어 학습
끊어 읽기 표시에 주의하면서 CD를 듣고, 큰 소리로 따라 읽습니다. 꼭 기억해야 할 단어들은 그림사전 형태로 제시되어 있습니다.

Tuesday
Words & Phrases 의미구 학습
단어와 명사구, 형용사구, 부사구, 전치사구 등 유용한 의미구를 연습해 봅니다. 듣기, 읽기, 쓰기 3단계의 학습이 익숙해지는 중요한 훈련입니다. Activity는 단어의 뜻과 철자(Spelling)를 연습하는 문제입니다.

Wednesday
Main Sentences 주요 문장 학습
중심 의미를 담고 있는 통문장 위주로 연습합니다. 이 문장들만으로도 전체 이야기를 말할 수 있답니다. 중심 문장만 따라서 완벽하게 말하고 쓸 수 있도록 지도해 주세요.

Thursday
Whole Story 전체 이야기 학습
우선, 전체 이야기를 CD로 들려주세요. 그 다음에 해석을 보면서 동시에 소리 내어 CD 따라 읽기(Shadow Reading)를 합니다. 어느 정도 빠른 스피드로 자연스럽게 따라 읽기가 되면, 전체 이야기를 다시 들으면서 따라 써 봅니다.

Friday
Fill in the blanks 빈 칸 채우기
끊어 읽기 표시와 해석 도움 없이, 전체 이야기를 들으면서 빈칸을 채워나가는 활동입니다. 잘 듣지 못 했다고 해서 중간에 멈춰 여러 번 듣지 않도록 해 주세요. 끝까지 다 마친 후에, 스스로 검토(Proofreading)하면서 고쳐나갈 수 있도록 하고 다시 들려주는 방식으로 진행합니다. Activity는 문법 문제입니다.

Saturday
Weekly Test 확인 학습
어휘, 내용 이해에 관한 문제들이 통합적으로 출제됩니다. 정리 학습에 아주 유용할 거예요.

Step 3: Review

Remind the Story
이야기 되새겨 보기
익숙해진 이야기를 아이들 스스로의 단어를 이용하여 써 보는 곳입니다. 주어진 해석도 영어 어순에 따르지 않은 자연스런 우리말이랍니다. 아이가 약간 다른 표현법과 단어를 이용했다면 오히려 칭찬해 주세요.

-THE END-

The Ant and the Grasshopper

This book belongs to ___________

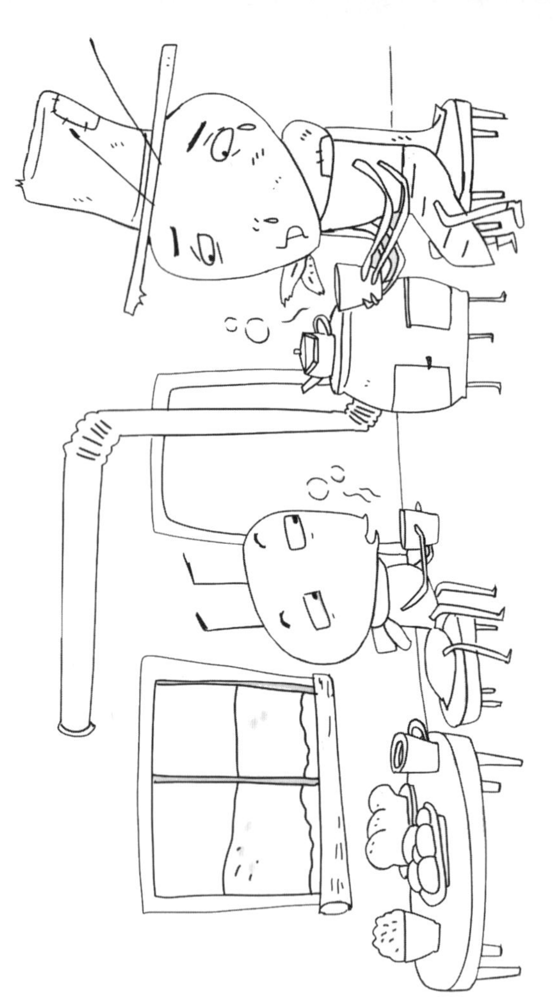

The ant gives him warm food and hot drink.

"Thank you, my friend," says the grasshopper.

"Now, I learned an important thing.

I will work hard in the summer, too."

The grasshopper is deeply sorry.

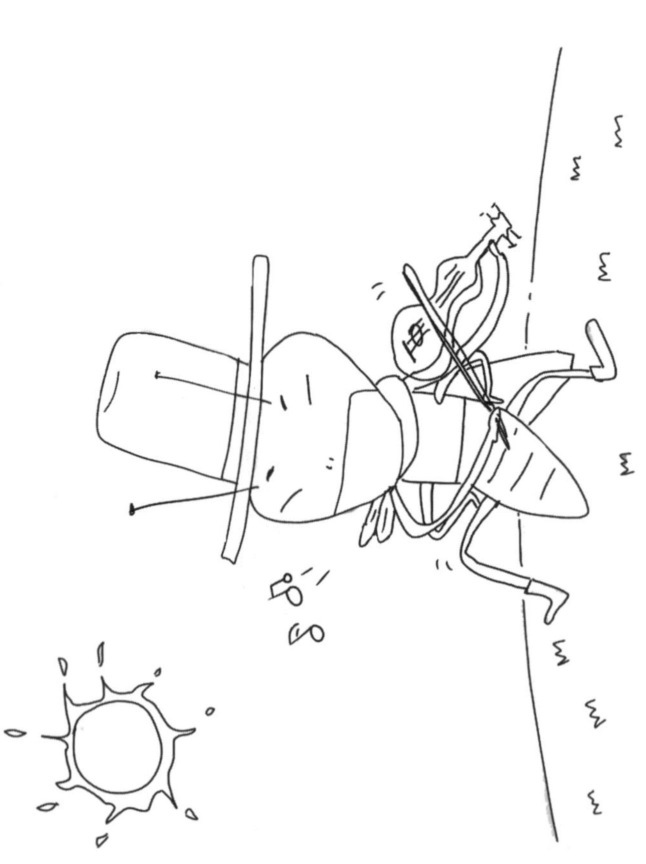

It is summer.

The weather is nice.

Here is a grasshopper in the field.

The grasshopper jumps

and sings and dances.

He plays all day long.

The ant is in her house.
She is warm and happy.
She has lots of food in her house.
She sees the grasshopper outside.
"Oh, poor thing. I should help him,"
says the ant.

The weather is getting hot.
Here is an ant in the field.
The ant finds food.
She is busy gathering grain.
She works hard all day long.

"Hey, stop working! Come and sing with me."

"No, I can't. Winter is coming soon.

You also should work hard," says the ant.

"Don't be silly! The summer is long."

The grasshopper laughs at the ant.

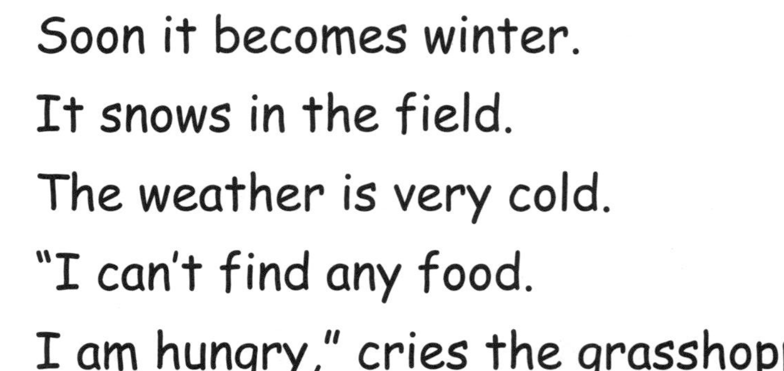

Soon it becomes winter.

It snows in the field.

The weather is very cold.

"I can't find any food.

I am hungry," cries the grasshopper.